FOR DAVID, BITSY, AND
THEIR DAUGHTERS

SIMON & SCHUSTER BOOKS FOR YOUNG READERS
An imprint of Simon & Schuster Children's Publishing Division
1230 Avenue of the Americas
New York, New York 10020

Text copyright © 1998 by Carole Armstrong
For photographic acknowledgments and copyright details, see pages 42–45

First published in Great Britain in 1998 by Frances Lincoln Limited
First U.S. edition 1998

The text in this book is set in Perpetua.

Printed and bound in Hong Kong
1 3 5 7 9 10 8 6 4 2

Library of Congress Cataloging-in-Publication Data

Armstrong, Carole
Women of the Bible / by Carole Armstrong.
p.   cm.
Summary: Presents the stories of prominent women from the Bible, including
Eve, Sarah, Bathsheba, Ruth, Mary, Elisabeth and Martha.
ISBN 0-689-81728-2
1. Women in the Bible—Biography—Juvenile literature. [Women in the Bible]
I. Title.
BS575.A76   1998
220.9'2082—dc21
97–17059
CIP
AC

WOMEN of the BIBLE

WITH PAINTINGS FROM THE GREAT ART MUSEUMS OF THE WORLD

CAROLE ARMSTRONG

SIMON & SCHUSTER
BOOKS FOR YOUNG READERS

AUTHOR'S NOTE

THROUGHOUT history, women of the Bible have been featured as symbols of courage and strength. Several of them were great leaders and important figures in their community, while others, from more humble origins, are remembered for their virtue and humility. Regardless of their background or status, each woman has a story to tell.

On many occasions the women of the Bible act out of loyalty to their kin: Susanna prefers to face death rather than be unfaithful to her husband, and Esther, too, is prepared to sacrifice her life for her people. Others use their charm and beauty to influence the outcome of events in their favor: Salome cunningly tricks King Herod into beheading her mother's enemy, and Delilah exploits her hold over her lover, Samson, to find out the secret of his strength. Whatever their story, each woman's experience is of value for us today.

Many artists over the centuries have been inspired to paint these women. Whether in domestic or grandiose settings, they radiate an independence of spirit, and the glorious paintings are a tribute to their legacy.

✳

CONTENTS

EVE

"And the rib, which the Lord God had taken from man, made he a woman, and brought her unto the man."
(Genesis 2:22)

EVE, the first woman, was created by God from one of Adam's ribs. As Adam's wife, she lived in the Garden of Eden alongside God's other creatures. The Garden provided all they could wish for and they had to obey only one rule: not to eat the fruit from the Tree of Knowledge of Good and Evil. If they disobeyed, God told Adam, they would die.

Every day Eve wandered in the garden playing with the animals and picking delicious fruits. One afternoon, as she sat down to rest under the Tree of Knowledge, she heard a hiss. She looked up and saw a serpent hanging from a branch. He invited her to taste one of the golden fruits from the Tree—after all, she was allowed to eat anything she liked. Although tempted, Eve shook her head: This was the one fruit forbidden by God. The serpent persisted: "God doth know that in the day ye eat thereof ye shall be as gods, knowing good and evil," he said persuasively.

Eve was even more tempted by the thought that the fruit would make her wise. Unable to resist, she stealthily picked one, and ran to find Adam. When she saw him, she told him what the serpent had said, and together they ate the fruit. Then, afraid that God would discover what they had done, they hid in the bushes.

In the evening, God summoned Adam and Eve to appear before Him. He saw that they had covered their bodies with fig leaves, ashamed of their nakedness, and He realized that they must have eaten the fruit from the Tree of Knowledge. He was angry with Eve for listening to the serpent, and with both of them for disobeying Him. They were punished by having to leave the Garden of Eden forever, and Eve was told that she would suffer in childbirth. Nevertheless, she became the mother of humankind, bearing three sons, Cain, Abel, and Seth.

In Cranach's painting, Eve has taken a bite from the fruit and the snake watches her from the tree. The artist uses light to make her stand out against the dark background.

HAGAR and SARAH

*"And the angel of God called to Hagar out of heaven, and said unto her,
'What aileth thee, Hagar? Fear not.'"* (Genesis 21:17)

SARAH was the wife of Abraham, forefather of the people of Israel. After many years of marriage, she was still childless. Desperate for her husband's line to continue, she encouraged him to have a child with Hagar, her Egyptian slave-girl.

As soon as Hagar became pregnant, she began to despise Sarah: Why should she, the mother of Abraham's child, continue to serve as a slave? Angered by Hagar's defiance, Sarah treated her harshly. Hagar became bitterly unhappy and decided to flee to the desert.

There, an angel of the Lord appeared to her. He urged her to return to her life with Abraham and Sarah, but promised that her unborn child would become a powerful leader: "I will multiply thy seed exceedingly." Comforted by the angel's words, Hagar returned to Abraham and Sarah. Soon after, her son Ishmael was born.

Many years later, when Sarah was very old, God blessed her with a son called Isaac. Sarah was afraid that Ishmael would rob Isaac of his inheritance, and she tried to persuade Abraham to banish him and his mother. Abraham loved both his sons, but God reminded him that Isaac was the one destined to be the leader of his children, and encouraged him to listen to Sarah. As for Ishmael, God would take care of him. With a heavy heart, Abraham sent Hagar and Ishmael into the desert.

Without any sign of water or shelter, Hagar gave way to despair: "Let me not see the death of the child," she wept. No sooner were her words spoken than the angel of the Lord appeared and pointed to a well close by, full of water. Hagar and Ishmael were saved and continued to live in the desert until Ishmael reached manhood.

Although Sarah and Hagar were rivals, they were treated equally by God. Both their sons became great leaders—Ishmael of the Arab peoples, and Isaac of the Jews.

The artist Sacchi paints Hagar and Ishmael in the desert. Ishmael is bathed in a strong light, contrasting with the softer treatment of his mother and the angel.

REBEKAH

"Drink, and I will give thy camels drink also."
(Genesis 24:46)

REBEKAH was an Israelite, and a distant relative of Abraham. She lived with her family in Nahor, where Abraham was born and spent his childhood.

After the death of his wife, Abraham was concerned about his son, Isaac: He did not want him to marry a Canaanite, but wished to find him a wife of his own kin. He instructed his servant, Eliezer, to go to Nahor and find a wife there for Isaac.

Soon after, Eliezer set off on his journey. As evening fell he reached the outskirts of Nahor where he stopped beside a well. Girls from the city had gathered to draw water, and Eliezer prayed to God that one of them would offer him a drink: "Let the same be the woman whom the Lord hath appointed out for my master's son," he said, hoping that he could soon return to Abraham having fulfilled his task.

Rebekah was one of the girls standing by the well. Eliezer was struck by her beauty and approached her: "Let me drink, I pray thee," he said. Rebekah dutifully offered to share her pitcher and then to water his camels. Curious to know who she was, Eliezer asked about her family. When he learned that she was related to Nahor, Abraham's brother, he could barely believe his luck. He went to meet her father Bethuel, and after bestowing gifts upon her family, Eliezer explained how he had journeyed from Canaan to find Isaac a wife. Now that he had met Rebekah, he could return. Although sad at the thought of losing his daughter, Bethuel saw that it was God's will she should marry Isaac: "Take her, and go, and let her be thy master's son's wife, as the Lord hath spoken," he said.

Isaac took Rebekah as his wife, and loved her. Several years later, she bore him twins, Esau and Jacob.

This image by Poussin is composed in a classical style with the girls posing as if in an ancient frieze. Eliezer and Rebekah dominate the foreground. The clear evening light illuminates the figures and casts long, dark shadows over the landscape.

RACHEL and LEAH

"Leah was tender eyed; but Rachel was beautiful and well favored. And Jacob loved Rachel."
(Genesis 29:17–18)

RACHEL and LEAH lived with their father, Laban, a shepherd in Haran. When Jacob, the son of Isaac, arrived in Haran to marry one of Laban's daughters, he immediately fell in love with Rachel, the younger and prettier of the girls. Laban said Jacob could marry her provided he worked for seven years as an unpaid shepherd. As time passed, Jacob's love for Rachel grew. Leah, on the other hand, remained unmarried, and Laban began to fear that despite her good character, she would never find a husband.

At last the wedding day arrived. After the celebrations the bride was led into the darkened chamber where Jacob was waiting. Only when morning came did he discover to his fury that his bride was not Rachel, but Leah. When he demanded his rightful wife, Laban pretended that it was customary to marry the eldest daughter first. Reluctantly, Jacob agreed to work another seven years to claim the woman he loved.

Leah bore Jacob many sons, but Rachel seemed unable to have children. As the years passed, she became sad and very jealous of her sister, afraid that Jacob would stop loving her. Leah was just as jealous, because she knew that Jacob preferred Rachel despite her barrenness. Secretly Leah hoped that by having Jacob's children, he would come to love her too.

Eventually, "God remembered Rachel," and she gave birth to Joseph, Jacob's favorite son. He was a man of virtue and wisdom, and became Pharaoh's chief minister. Tragically, Rachel died giving birth to a second son, Benjamin.

Here Rossetti paints Leah in a green gown, the color of life. Rachel is looking melancholy; she is wearing purple, a color the artist associated with death. The tiny figure in the background represents Dante, the great poet much admired by Rossetti.

DEBORAH

"Awake, awake, Deborah! Awake, awake, utter a song."
(Judges 5:12)

DEBORAH was a great judge of Israel, the only woman ever to have held such a position. Many people flocked to hear her wise words as she delivered her judgments on Mount Ephraim, sitting under a palm tree, the tree of life and a symbol of hope.

At this time, the Israelites were ruled by the Canaanites who were led by a general called Sisera. He was a powerful man and for twenty years he had oppressed the Israelites. Eventually the Israelite leaders came to Deborah in the hope that she could rescue them from their plight. Knowing that she could rely on God's help, Deborah immediately summoned Barak, military commander of the Israelites, and ordered him to gather together ten thousand men. She reminded him of God's command to lead his people to Mount Tabor and fight Sisera's army. Barak was afraid—Sisera had nine hundred chariots of iron and an army that far outnumbered his. "If thou wilt go with me," he told Deborah, "then I will go." Deborah agreed, for she had God's promise that the Israelites would win: "I will draw unto thee Sisera, with his chariots and his multitude; and I will deliver him into thine hand," she assured Barak, and before long, the Israelites defeated Sisera's army.

Sisera was forced to escape on foot and took refuge in the tent of a friend called Heber. Jael, Heber's wife, pretended to welcome the General, but secretly she sympathized with the Israelites. When he feel asleep, she brutally killed him with a blow to his head.

From that day, the Israelites were free from oppression. Deborah composed a beautiful song of triumph and praise to God, as it was with His help that the Israelites had overthrown the Canaanites.

Solimena, a Neapolitan artist, paints Deborah sitting on her throne, commanding Barak to go into battle. Above Barak's head is a winged figure holding a palm leaf of victory and a laurel wreath which symbolizes triumph and eternity.

DELILAH

"And she made him sleep upon her knees; and she called for a man, and she caused him to shave off the seven locks of his head. . . and his strength went from him." (Judges 16:19)

DELILAH lived in the valley of Sorek, an area ruled by the Philistines with whom she had strong links. Samson, her lover, had become a hero among the Israelites during the wars against the Philistines. He was a giant of a man, with long hair, and he performed many acts of strength. On one occasion, he destroyed thousands of Philistines using the jawbone of an ass as his only weapon.

When Samson fell in love with Delilah, the Philistines saw a chance to capture him. Each Philistine leader offered Delilah eleven hundred pieces of silver if she could find out the secret of Samson's strength. The challenge and the huge reward excited her.

First, Delilah tried to trick Samson by tying him up with strong ropes, but he broke free as easily as if they were cotton threads. She soon saw that the most powerful weapon she had was Samson's passion for her. "How canst thou say 'I love thee,' when thine heart is not with me?" she pleaded. "Thou hast mocked me and hast not told me wherein thy great strength lieth."

Eventually Samson gave in and told Delilah that since his birth, his hair had never been cut—if it was, he would lose his God-given strength. Hiding her triumph, Delilah soothed Samson to sleep, resting him across her knees. Then she told the Philistines to hide and watch while a servant quietly cut her lover's hair. Samson's strength ebbed away, the Philistines seized him, and Delilah claimed the reward for her trickery.

Delilah's story illustrates how feminine wiles can conquer masculine strength. Cranach suggests her power over Samson by painting her, rather than a servant, cutting his hair, while a Philistine hides in the bushes, waiting. Ironically, Samson is still clutching the jawbone of an ass—a symbol of his strength. The couple's elaborate clothes and the landscape in the background illustrate Cranach's attention to detail.

R U T H and N A O M I

"Whither thou goest, I will go; and where thou lodgest, I will lodge:
thy people shall be my people, and thy God my God." (Ruth 1:16)

NAOMI and her husband had moved from Bethlehem to Moab where their two sons married local girls, Ruth and Orpah. Their life there came to a tragic end, however, with the deaths of Naomi's husband and sons. Poor and desolate, Naomi decided to return to Israel. She urged Ruth and Orpah to stay behind, but Ruth loved Naomi and refused to abandon her.

The two women arrived in Bethlehem at the time of the barley harvest. Ruth found work on the land of a rich and powerful man called Boaz, a relative of Naomi. Boaz soon noticed the stranger at work in his fields. He invited her to share his servants' food and drink, and encouraged his reapers to throw corn her way as she worked. Ruth was puzzled by his kindness, but Boaz knew of her devotion to Naomi and had seen that she was a hard worker. He wanted to help her.

Before long, Naomi saw that Boaz was growing fond of Ruth and began to think of how she could encourage a marriage between them.

One night she sent Ruth to lie at Boaz's feet while he was sleeping. It was past midnight when he awoke, startled to find Ruth apparently guarding him. Following Naomi's instructions, Ruth asked Boaz to spread his cloak over her—according to ancient custom, if he did this, it meant that her property became his, and he, in turn, would marry and protect her. Boaz was flattered by the fact that Ruth had chosen him above any other man, and he gently covered her with his cloak.

Soon after, Boaz and Ruth were married, and they had a son called Obed. Living with them and caring for their child, Naomi found happiness again.

The artist, a follower of Jan van Scorel, suggests the importance of Ruth and Naomi by painting them in the foreground. Ruth's elaborate dress contrasts with the muted tones of the landscape.

ABIGAIL

"She was a woman of good understanding, and of a beautiful countenance."
(I Samuel 25:3)

ABIGAIL lived in the valley of Jezreel, at the foot of Mount Carmel, with her husband, Nabal, a wealthy farmer. Abigail was clever and beautiful, but her husband was known for his coarse, rude manner.

In the days before he became King of Israel, David was traveling through the desert with his men. It was the sheep-shearing season, a time of festivity, and David expected Nabal to offer him hospitality. Instead, the farmer turned him away, refusing to feed or entertain his men. David was furious and swore to take revenge on Nabal and his household.

Abigail heard what had happened and realized that she would have to move quickly if she was going to save her boorish husband. Secretly she loaded her donkeys and camels with bread, fruit, meat, and wine and set off to find David.

As soon as she found him, Abigail threw herself at his feet and begged him to have mercy on Nabal. She said that she was to blame for her husband's behavior—he was a fool who knew no better. She offered David gifts and praised his noble character. Surely, she said, a clear conscience would serve him better than an act of vengeance, and would be better rewarded by God? Won over by her eloquence and beauty, David agreed to spare Nabal's life.

Abigail went home to find Nabal in a drunken stupor. Next morning, she told him what had happened. Ten days later, God freed Abigail from her burdensome husband: "The Lord smote Nabal, that he died." When David heard of Nabal's death, he sent for Abigail and married her.

The Spanish artist Escalante paints Abigail—peacemaker and symbol of the victory of diplomacy—kneeling at David's feet, surrounded by gifts. The dark color of the bull emphasizes her pallor, suggesting her fear as she begs for her husband's life.

BATHSHEBA

"He saw a woman washing herself; and the woman was very beautiful to look upon."
(II Samuel 11:2)

BATHSHEBA lived in Jerusalem with her husband Uriah, during the reign of King David. One day, when she was bathing in a courtyard close to the palace, King David saw her from a rooftop. Stunned by her beauty, he summoned her to the palace. Bathsheba was taken aback by the King's request, but obeyed without question. Face-to-face, David found her even more irresistible, and he became determined to marry her. David secretly arranged to have Bathsheba's husband, Uriah, killed in battle. Bathsheba grieved when she heard about Uriah's death, but accepted her new role as the King's wife.

Several months later, she bore David a son. Her new happiness, however, was short-lived. God was angry with the King for killing Uriah and wanted to punish him: Seven days later, the newborn baby died. Bathsheba was distraught—she had now lost her son and her first husband—but it was not long before God took mercy upon her. She soon had a second son called Solomon.

Many years later, Bathsheba's loyalty to David was rewarded. She wanted Solomon to succeed David as King, and when his claim to the throne was threatened, she reminded David of a promise he had made her: "Assuredly, Solomon thy son shall reign after me." Moved by her heartfelt appeal, he granted her wish and proclaimed Solomon the King of Israel. Bathsheba had not only protected her son's interests, but her actions had assured the people of Israel of a great leader who ruled with wisdom for many years to come.

In this detailed painting by Krodel, Bathsheba, dressed in elaborate clothes, is washing her feet while King David serenades her with his harp.

E S T H E R

"If it please the king, let my life be given me at my petition, and my people at my request."
(Esther 7:3)

ESTHER was a poor Jewish orphan who lived with her uncle Mordecai in Persia. Ahasuerus, the King of Persia, wanted to find a new queen, and he invited young women from all over the land to come and live at the palace for a year so that he could choose among them. Mordecai encouraged Esther to accept the King's offer.

Her simple beauty conquered the heart of Ahasuerus, and he made her his queen. On Mordecai's advice, however, Esther concealed the fact that she was Jewish.

At the King's court lived an evil, powerful man called Haman. When Mordecai refused to bow to him—it was against his principles to bow to anyone but God— Haman plotted to destroy him and the whole Jewish community. Mordecai pleaded with Esther to persuade Ahasuerus to be merciful to her people. He reminded her that she too was Jewish—if Haman's plot succeeded, she would have to choose between death or renouncing her heritage and remaining Queen.

Taking her life in her hands—the punishment for entering the King's presence without his permission could be death—Esther put on her richest robes and crown, and approached Ahasuerus, pale and trembling. Disarmed by her beauty, the King offered her anything she wanted. She confessed that she was Jewish, and told him about the plot against her people. Ahasuerus was horrified, and as punishment, Haman was hanged on the gallows he had ordered built for Mordecai. Mordecai, on the other hand, received honors and riches, and the Jewish community was saved.

In the central panel of this triptych (a painting with three panels), the Flemish painter Herri met de Bles shows Esther kneeling before Ahasuerus, asking for mercy on her people. The decoration of the palace and the richly patterned clothes of Esther and the King show the artist's detailed style, typical of Flemish painting. The perspective of the painting draws our eye through the palace arches to the townscape background.

JUDITH

"There is not such a woman from one end of the earth to the other, both for beauty of face, and wisdom of words." (APOCRYPHA, Judith 11:21)

JUDITH lived in the Jewish town of Bethulia when it was beseiged by the Assyrian army led by General Holofernes. The town's water supply had been cut off and the situation was desperate. Knowing that within a matter of days they would have no alternative, the elders of the city decided to surrender.

Judith was horrified—giving in to the enemy went against God's will. Trusting in God to help her, and determined to save her people, she persuaded the elders to let her set off with her maid to the enemy camp. When she reached it, she tricked the Assyrian guards into taking her to see Holofernes.

The General listened fascinated as she told him that her people had broken sacred laws and were to be punished by God. She, as Holofernes' servant, would ensure their destruction: Each night she would pray, and God would tell her when the time was right to attack the Jewish city, and then she would tell Holofernes. The General never doubted her sincerity, and thought she was sure to bring him victory.

On her fourth day in the camp, Holofernes invited Judith to dine with him. At the meal he drank heavily, and soon afterwards he fell asleep. Judith saw her opportunity and seized it. Stealthily she took his sword. With a prayer to God to give her strength, she grabbed his hair and, with two mighty strokes, cut off his head. She hid the head in her maid's food bag, and quickly escaped.

The townspeople could hardly believe it when Judith returned to Bethulia with Holofernes' head. Instead of surrendering, they fought and defeated the Assyrians.

The Venetian painter Giorgione shows Judith elegantly dressed, holding a sword, her foot resting delicately on Holofernes' head. By painting her with her eyes modestly downcast, the artist encourages us to focus on her beauty and courage rather than on the horror of her actions.

SUSANNA

"Oh everlasting God, that knowest the secrets. Thou knowest that they have borne false witness against me."
(APOCRYPHA, The History of Susanna 42–43)

SUSANNA was married to a wealthy man called Joakim. She was well-educated and known for her grace and beauty. Because the couple lived in a huge house, elders of the city—men with a reputation for wisdom and virtue—came there to deliver judgments to the people. Two of them noticed Susanna taking her daily walk in the gardens. Overwhelmed by her beauty, they planned to seduce her.

One hot day, Susanna decided to bathe in the garden. Unaware that the elders were spying on her from the bushes, she sent her maids to fetch bath oils and shut the gate so that she could undress in private. The elders saw their chance and sprang from the bushes: "We are in love with thee; therefore consent unto us, and lie with us," they said, warning her that if she did not agree, they would tell Joakim she had been secretly meeting another man. Susanna was trapped: She did not want to be unfaithful to her husband, but unless she did as the elders wanted, her fate was sealed. No one would believe her word against theirs and she would be condemned to death. However, Susanna refused to give in to them: She would rather die than "sin in the sight of the Lord."

The next day the elders carried out their threat: In front of her husband, they accused Susanna of adultery. Joakim believed them and Susanna was condemned to death. As she was being led to her execution, she prayed for God's help. He heard her prayer and chose a man called Daniel to save her: "Are ye such fools, ye sons of Israel, that without examination or knowledge of the truth ye have condemned a daughter of Israel?" he cried, and demanded the chance to question the elders separately. When their stories did not match, it became obvious that they were lying. Susanna's name was cleared and the elders were sent for execution.

Jacopo da Empoli emphasizes Susanna's modesty and humility by painting her seated with her eyes downcast and her face half-hidden in the shadows.

ELISABETH

"And thy wife Elisabeth shall bear thee a son, and thou shalt call his name John."
(Luke 1:13)

ELISABETH was married to a priest called Zacharias. One day, when Zacharias was carrying out his duties in the temple, the angel Gabriel appeared to him. He told Zacharias that Elisabeth would bear a son, and they must name him John. Zacharias found this difficult to believe—Elisabeth was barren and he thought that he was too old to have a child. Because Zacharias was without faith, Gabriel struck him dumb "until the day that these things shall be performed." Unable to speak, he hurried home to his wife.

Shortly after, Elisabeth conceived, just as the angel had said. She could barely believe that she was to have a child, and she spent the next five months quietly at home, praising God. Mary, her cousin who was pregnant with Jesus, came to visit her. As soon as Elisabeth heard Mary's voice, she felt the baby stir in her womb for the first time. She saw this as a sign of the holiness of Mary and her baby, and she was filled with joy. Mary stayed with Elisabeth, and was a loving companion to the older woman during her pregnancy.

Soon after Mary left, Elisabeth gave birth to a son. Elisabeth insisted that he be called John. Zacharias confirmed this choice by writing the name on a tablet, and immediately he was able to speak again. John grew up to be Jesus' closest disciple and proclaimed him the Messiah. He earned the name John the Baptist after baptizing repentant sinners.

The meeting between Elisabeth and Mary is called "The Visitation" and is a favorite subject for artists. Here, Ghirlandaio shows his mastery of light and color. He depicts the tenderness between the two women by painting Elisabeth in a golden, yellow robe kneeling at Mary's feet, praising her holiness. Behind them is a peaceful harbor, framed by the classical buildings.

MARY, MOTHER OF JESUS

"And the angel said unto her, 'Fear not, Mary: for thou hast found favour with God.'"
(Luke 1:30)

MARY, a young virgin, lived in the town of Nazareth. She was betrothed to a carpenter called Joseph. One day, she was quietly reading at home when the angel Gabriel appeared to her, sent by God with a message. Mary was alarmed, but Gabriel told her not to be afraid: She would soon give birth to a son called Jesus. Mary, who was not yet married to Joseph, was puzzled: "How shall this be?" she asked. The angel explained that she would conceive the child of the Holy Ghost and that, "He shall be called the Son of God."

Several weeks later, Mary went to visit her cousin, Elisabeth, who was also pregnant. Elisabeth immediately sensed Mary's holiness: "Blessed art thou among women, and blessed is the fruit of thy womb," she proclaimed. Hearing her cousin's words, Mary's faith in God grew strong: "My soul doth magnify the Lord, and my spirit hath rejoiced in God my Savior," she sang in wonder. Mary then returned to Nazareth and her life with Joseph.

Soon after, the Emperor ordered everyone to go back to their birthplace to be taxed. Joseph was one of David's descendants, which meant he and Mary had to travel to Bethlehem. The town was crowded and there was nowhere for them to stay. It was almost time for Mary to give birth, and in desperation, Joseph persuaded an innkeeper to let them shelter in his stables. There, Jesus was born, surrounded by animals. Mary wrapped him in swaddling clothes and laid him in a manger. She was filled with joy as she gazed at her miraculous son.

Filippo Lippi frames Mary in a window set above a landscape; angels hold the baby Jesus up to her. The figures form a triangular shape conveying a feeling of harmony and stability. The artist emphasizes Mary's youthful beauty by bathing her face in a soft light.

HERODIAS
and SALOME

"Whatsoever thou shalt ask of me, I will give it thee, unto the half of my kingdom."
(Mark 6:23)

HERODIAS, a powerful Queen, was the wife of King Herod. Many people disapproved of their marriage because she had divorced her first husband, King Herod's own brother, by whom she had a daughter, Salome. John the Baptist, a popular and devout holy man, angered the Queen by publicly condemning her. She wanted him put to death, but Herod respected John for his honorable conduct and protected him from Herodias.

It was King Herod's birthday and Salome, his stepdaughter, was persuaded to dance at the celebration banquet. The King was bewitched by her spellbinding performance, and without stopping to think, offered her anything she wanted as a reward.

Salome did not know what to ask for, and looked for advice to her mother. At last Herodias saw a chance to take revenge on her old enemy. She whispered instructions in her daughter's ear, and when Salome went back to the King she told him: "I will that thou give me by and by in a charger the head of John the Baptist."

The King was aghast, but he had made the promise to Salome in front of his guests and he had to keep his word. He sent an executioner to behead the innocent man. When a guard brought the head in on a platter, Herodias smiled. She had her revenge at last.

Salome is painted by Gozzoli with her arms in a seductive pose as she dances for King Herod. The artist uses brilliant light and shadow on her clothes to express the movement of the dance. In the background, dressed in a red robe, a color which suggests danger, we see Herodias receiving the head of John the Baptist from her daughter.

MARTHA and MARY

"Now Jesus loved Martha, and her sister, and Lazarus."
(John 11: 5)

MARTHA and **MARY** were sisters of Lazarus, a follower of Jesus. Although close, the sisters were different in character: Mary was a dreamer, content to be alone, while Martha loved company and bustled around the house taking charge of everyone.

One evening, Jesus came to visit them. Each sister showed in her own way what a pleasure it was to welcome him. Martha busied herself preparing his meal, but Mary, instead of helping her sister, sat at his feet, hanging on every word he spoke. Martha was hurt and angry that she was the one doing all the work: "Lord dost thou not care that my sister hath left me to serve alone?" she asked. Jesus answered her kindly, but refused to scold Mary: While Martha had been busy, her sister had been listening intently to his teachings, and his words would stay with her forever.

Not long afterwards, Lazarus became ill—so ill that his sisters were afraid he would die. Knowing of the miracles Jesus had worked, they sent a desperate message, begging him to come and save their brother. But Jesus waited, so Lazarus died before he arrived.

Distraught with grief, Martha and Mary took Jesus to the cave where they had laid their brother's body. Jesus told them to roll away the stone that blocked the entrance. At first Martha protested—he would smell awful as he had been dead four days—but Jesus told her that if she believed, she would see a miracle. When the stone was rolled clear, Jesus called to Lazarus to come out from the tomb. Seconds later, the dead man, still wrapped in his burial bandages, walked out alive.

Caravaggio uses his mastery of light and shade to emphasize the contrasting characters of the sisters: Martha, simply dressed and hidden in the shadows, reprimands Mary, whose elaborate dress is illuminated with brilliant color and light.

MARY MAGDALENE

"She hath washed my feet with tears, and wiped them with the hairs of her head."
(Luke 7:44)

MARY MAGDALENE lived in the fishing village of Magdala by the Sea of Galilee. Local people disapproved of her way of life, but Jesus treated her with compassion. On one occasion when she visited him, she showed her faith by bathing his feet with her tears and drying them with her hair, and she anointed and kissed them. Touched by her devotion, Jesus publicly forgave her sins: "Thy faith hath saved thee," he told her.

As one of the closest followers of Jesus, Mary witnessed his crucifixion. Grieving over her master's suffering and death, she visited his tomb two days later with spice and perfume to clean his body. To her amazement, the stone that had sealed the tomb was gone, and when she peered in she found that Jesus' body had disappeared. She went to tell the other disciples what had happened. They hurriedly came to the tomb to see for themselves if it were true, and after they left, she stayed behind. Alone again, Mary began to weep.

Suddenly two angels appeared: "Woman, why weepest thou?" they asked. As Mary explained, she became aware of a stranger standing behind her. She took him for a gardener and asked if he had removed the body, but then he spoke her name: "Mary..." She recognized his voice and fell to her knees—it was Jesus. He told her not to hold on to him, for he was not yet ascended to God, but assured her: "I ascend unto my Father, and your Father; and to my God, and your God." Filled with joy and love for her master, Mary ran to find the disciples and share the news with them.

Rogier van der Weyden's portrait of Mary was painted as part of a triptych. The artist conveys her sorrow by showing her tears. She holds the jar of ointment used to anoint Jesus' feet, which has become one of her symbols. The other is her long hair, used to dry her master's feet.

INDEX OF ARTISTS

COVER
Judith (detail)
SODOMA
1477-1549

Pinacoteca Nazionale, Siena

ENDPAPERS, TITLE PAGE AND BACK COVER
Queen of Sheba (detail)
PIERO DELLA FRANCESCA
1410-1492

S. Francesco, Arezzo

PAGE 9
Eve
LUCAS CRANACH,
THE ELDER
1472-1553

Uffizi, Florence

PAGE 10
Hagar and Ishmael in the Wilderness (detail)
ANDREA SACCHI
1599-1661

National Museum of Wales, Cardiff

PAGE 13
Eliezer and Rebekah (detail)
NICOLAS POUSSIN
1594-1665

Louvre, Paris

AND PAINTINGS

PAGE 15
Dante's Vision of Rachel and Leah (detail)
DANTE GABRIEL ROSSETTI
1828-1882

Tate Gallery, London

PAGE 17
Barak and Deborah (detail)
FRANCESCO SOLIMENA
1657-1747

Private collection

PAGE 23
The Prudent Abigail (detail)
JUAN ANTONIO ESCALANTE
c. 1630-1670

Prado, Madrid

PAGE 21
**Ruth and Naomi in the Field
of Boaz (detail)**
Panel
A FOLLOWER OF JAN VAN SCOREL
1495-1562

Kunsthistorisches Museum, Vienna

PAGE 18
Samson and Delilah (detail)
LUCAS CRANACH, THE ELDER
1472-1553

Staatsgalerie, Augsburg

PAGE 27
Esther and Ahasuerus (detail)
Triptych
HERRI MET DE BLES
c. 1500-1559 or 1560

Pinacoteca Nazionale, Bologna

PAGE 24
David and Bathsheba (detail)
Panel
WOLFGANG KRODEL
c. 1515-1561

Kunsthistorisches Museum, Vienna

PAGE 29
Judith (detail)
GIORGIONE
c. 1476 or 1478-1510

Hermitage, St. Petersburg

PAGE 31
Susanna in the Bath (detail)
JACOPO DA EMPOLI
1554-1640

Kunsthistorisches Museum, Vienna

PAGE 33
The Visitation (detail)
DOMENICO GHIRLANDAIO
1449-1494

Louvre, Paris

PAGE 34
Madonna and Child with Angels (detail)
FRA FILIPPO LIPPI
1406-1469

Uffizi, Florence

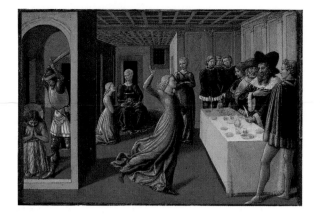

PAGE 36
The Dance of Salome (detail)
BENOZZO GOZZOLI
1420-1497

Samuel H. Kress Collection, National Gallery of Art,
Washington

PAGE 38
Martha reproving Mary for Her Vanity (detail)
CARAVAGGIO
1571-1610

Private Collection

PAGE 41
Saint Mary Magdalene (detail)
The Braque Family Triptych
ROGIER VAN DER WEYDEN
1399-1464

Louvre, Paris

✳

PHOTOGRAPHIC ACKNOWLEDGMENTS

For permission to reproduce the paintings on the following pages
and for supplying photographs, the publishers thank:

Art Resource, New York / Eric Lessing: **31**
Augsberg State Art Gallery: **18**
Bridgeman Art Library, London: **9, 17, 21, 23, 24, 29**
Christie's Images / Bridgeman Art Library, London: **38**
© **1997 Board of Trustees, National Gallery of Art,** Washington: **36**
National Museum of Wales, Cardiff: **10**
Pinacoteca Nazionale, Bologna: **27**
© **photo RMN,** Paris: **41**
Scala, Florence: **front cover, endpapers, title page, 5, 13, 33, 34, back cover**
Tate Gallery, London: **15**